All There Is To Know

© Flavia Publishers
All Rights Reserved

This

journal

is dedicated to

_____
_____
_____
_____
_____

Life doesn't come with a manual, it comes with a Mother.

My Life's Journey

Significant Milestones and Events that have shaped the person I am

My Life's Journey

Date

Date

Date

Date

Date

Date

My Life's Journey

Date

Date

Date

Date

Date

Date

My Life's Journey

Date

Date

Date

Date

Date

Date

My Life's Journey

Date

Date

Date

Date

Date

Date

My Life's Journey

Date

Date

Date

Date

Date

Date

My Life's Journey

Date

Date

Date

Date

Date

Date

My Life's Journey

Date	
Date	
Date	
Date	
Date	
Date	

My Life's Journey

Date

Date

Date

Date

Date

Date

My Life's Journey

Date

Date

Date

Date

Date

Date

My Life's Journey

Date

Date

Date

Date

Date

Date

My Life's Journey

Date

Date

Date

Date

Date

Date

My Life's Journey

Date

Date

Date

Date

Date

Date

My Life's Journey

Date

Date

Date

Date

Date

Date

My Life's Journey

Date

Date

Date

Date

Date

Date

My Life's Journey

Date

Date

Date

Date

Date

Date

My Life's Journey

Date

Date

Date

Date

Date

Date

My Life's Journey

Date

Date

Date

Date

Date

Date

My Life's Journey

Date

Date

Date

Date

Date

Date

Being a mother is learning about strengths you didn't know you had and dealing with fears you never knew existed.

~ Linda Wooten

When I was a child...

When I was a child...

I wanted to be a

When I was born I weighed

I was good at

My favorite

Color

Music

Food

When I was a child...

I wanted to be like

My best friend was

I had a crush on

My favorite Teacher

Move / TV Character

Me as a child

Me when I was younger

More about my early years

Mother's love
is peace.
It need not be acquired,
it need not be deserved.
~ Erich Fromm

Your father and me...

When I met
your father...

How I felt when I met him

We were at

I was wearing

Our first date was

As a couple...

Our favorite restaurant

"Our song"

Where we first lived

Nicknames

Your father and me

Your father and me

More about your father and me

A mother understands what a child does not say.
~ Jewish Proverb

About You...

When you were born...

Pregnancy cravings

I was in labor for

Our list of baby names

When I first held you, I felt...

When you were born...

Date

Time

Weight

When you were born...

Popular in that year

Song

Movie

Celebrity

Your pacifier was

You most enjoyed

We lived at

You as a baby

You as a toddler

Your Firsts and Favorites

First	Favorite
Steps	Baby food
Fall	Toy
Word	Song
Tantrum	Game
Friend	Movie
Pet	Outing

Your Firsts and Favorites

First	Favorite

Your Firsts and Favorites

First	Favorite

More about your early years

Moms are
the people
who know us the best
and love us the most.
~ Unknown

As your mother...

What being a mother means to me

what I love most about you

The times you've made me laugh

The times we've laughed together

The times I've felt your pain

The times you've made me proud

If I could give you anything...

Mother is a verb. It's something you do. Not just who you are.
~ Dorothy Canfield Fisher

Things that make me think of you

When I see…

When I hear...

When I touch…

When I smell…

When I taste…

Precious Memories

Sooner or later,
we all quote
our mothers.

~ Unknown

The best
advice
I could
give you

Facts and Fancies that might interest you

People who have influenced and impacted my life

If I could meet anyone, past or present, it would be...

A mother's love endures through all
~ Washington Irving

A moment in my life that made me...

Happy

Proud

Blush

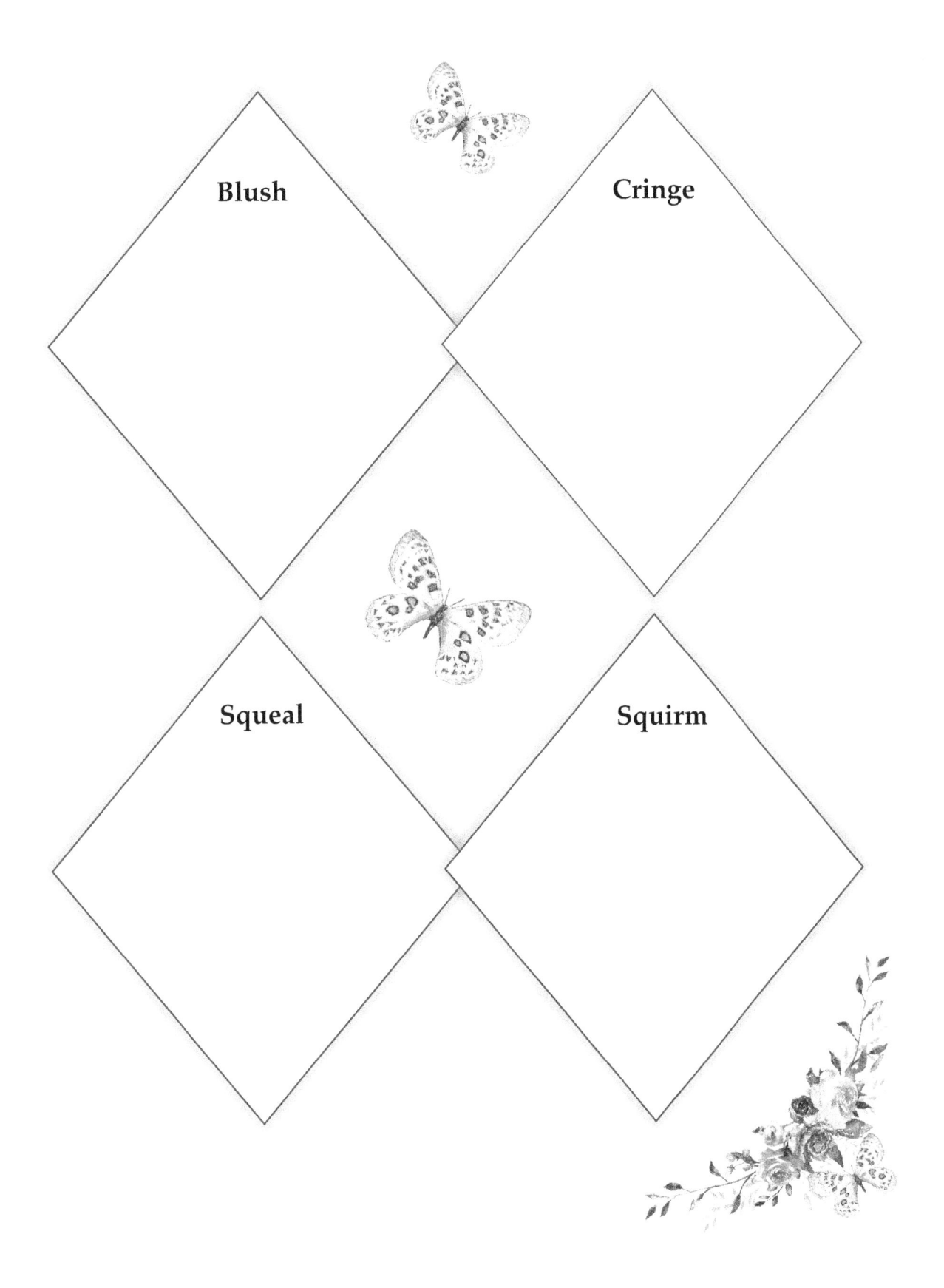

Cringe

Squeal

Squirm

Laugh

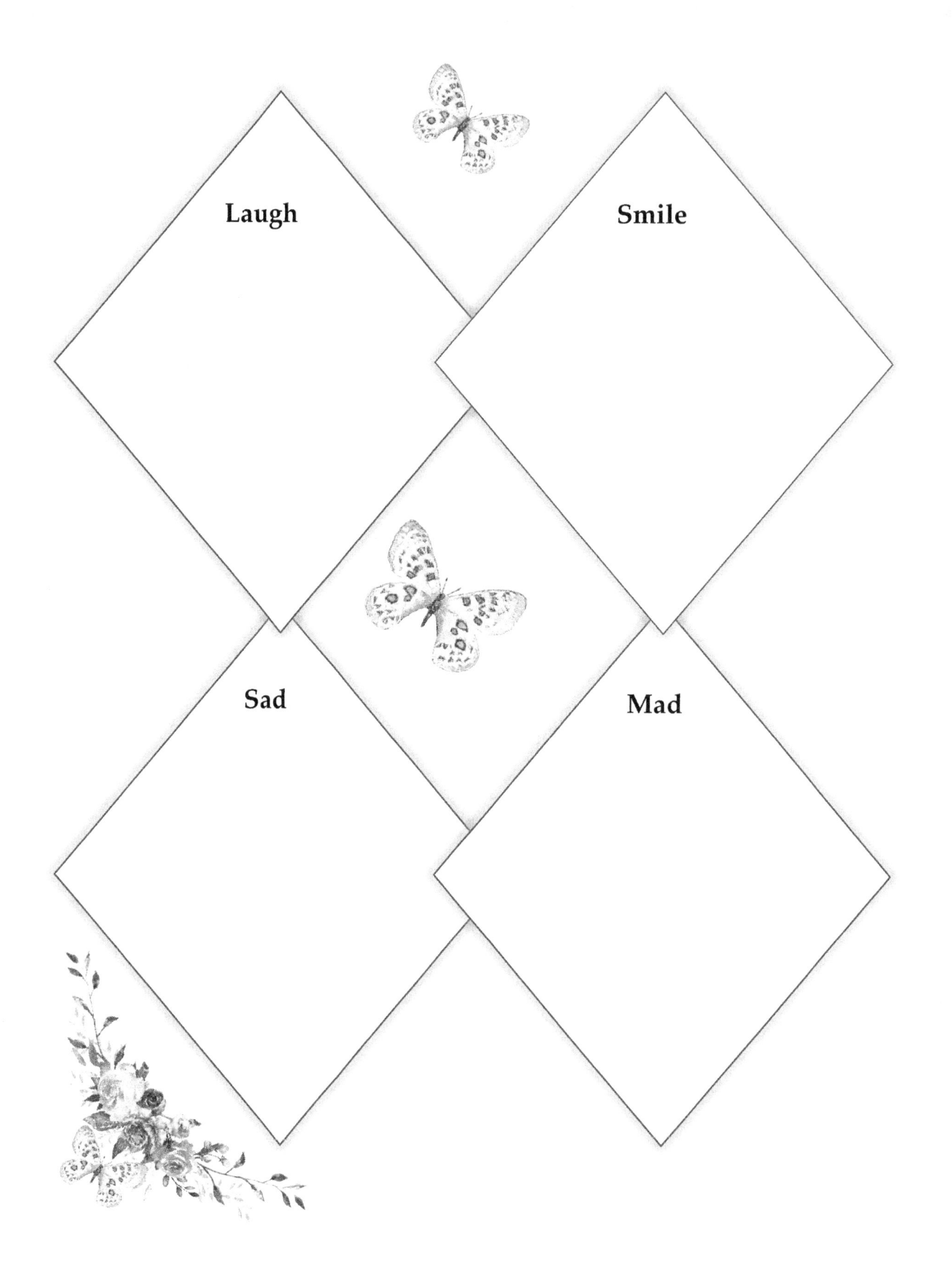

Smile

Sad

Mad

Blush

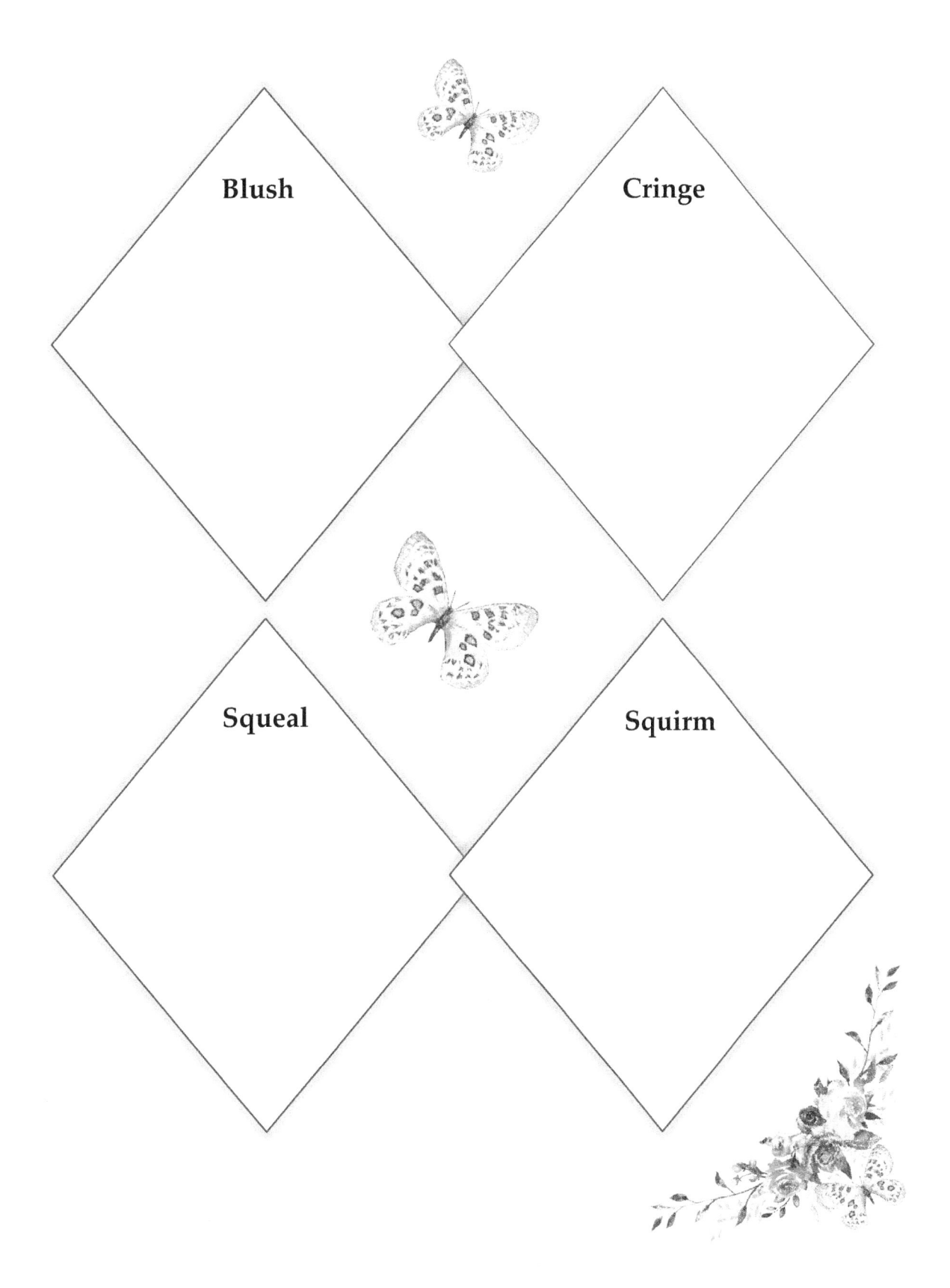

Cringe

Squeal

Squirm

Blush

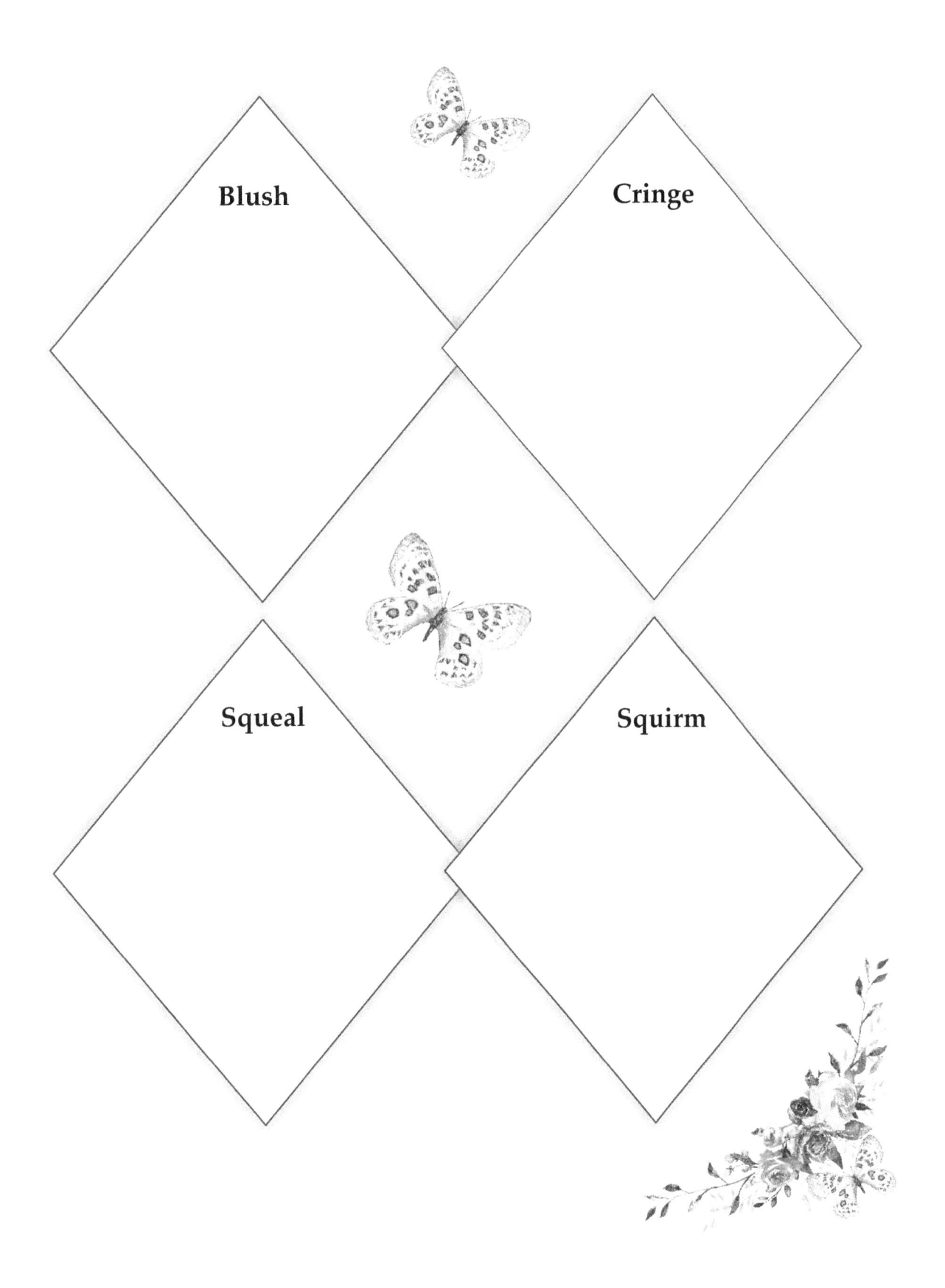

Cringe

Squeal

Squirm

I do these things because…

… I love to	… I have to

I do these things because...

... I love to   ... I have to

A mother's arms are more comforting than anyone else's

~ Princess Diana

© Flavia Publishers
All Rights Reserved

Made in the USA
Coppell, TX
16 May 2020